WELCOME TO THE MILLENNIUM, GEMINI

If you were born betweeen 22 May and 21 June, the 21st century is going to change quite a few things about the way you operate. As a Gemini, you tend to channel everything through your head, so get ready for a lot of analyzing . . .

If you look at the wheel (below), you can see just where your key zones are for the new millennium.

Love is obviously going to be a source of change. Meanwhile, Uranus and Neptune will be passing through your travel zone, which means you'll have some of the most exciting and inspiring times of your life in other regions or countries. Even if you never leave home, you might find the world comes to you!

But to find out more, turn the page. And don't forget your dates with destiny, starting on page 24.

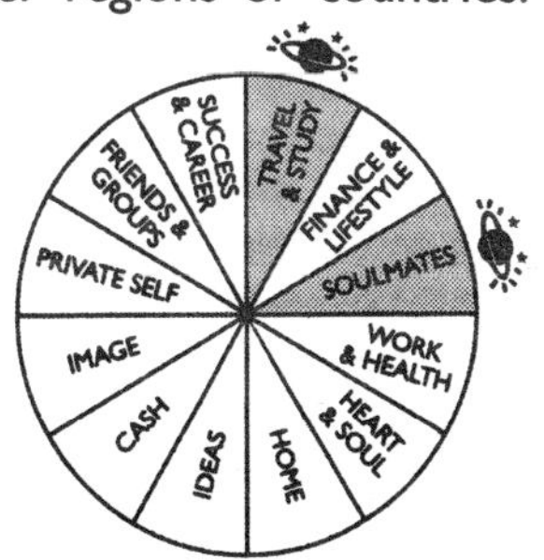

Jessica Adams

Handbag Horoscopes

Gemini

May 22–June 21

AN ONYX BOOK

ONYX
Published by New American Library, a division of
Penguin Putnam Inc., 375 Hudson Street,
New York, New York 10014, U.S.A.
Penguin Books Ltd, 27 Wrights Lane,
London W8 5TZ, England
Penguin Books Australia Ltd, Ringwood,
Victoria, Australia
Penguin Books Canada Ltd, 10 Alcorn Avenue,
Toronto, Ontario, Canada M4V 3B2
Penguin Books (N.Z.) Ltd, 182–190 Wairau Road,
Auckland 10, New Zealand

Penguin Books Ltd, Registered Offices:
Harmondsworth, Middlesex, England

Published by Onyx, an imprint of New American Library,
a division of Penguin Putnam Inc.
First published by Penguin Books Australia Ltd, 1999.

First Onyx Printing, November 2000
10 9 8 7 6 5 4 3

Printed in the United States of America

Acknowledgments

When I was seven years old, I read a book called *Catweazle and the Magic Zodiac*, by Richard Carpenter. Catweazle was a magician, and he was looking for the twelve star signs. In fact, he spent his entire time rushing around the English countryside on a tricycle, hunting them down.

As I was writing each Handbag Horoscope, I was reminded of Catweazle. And I would like to thank him for converting me to astrology at the age of seven. It was much more interesting than Barbie dolls, and it still is.

Handbag Horoscopes began as a scribbled idea on a notepad. Alison Cowan, Julie Gibbs and Gaby Naher turned the idea into something real. Thank you! I would also like to thank Electric Ephemeris and Adam Smith for their help with the tables.

Contents

ONE

Astrology Works—and Here's the Proof

Here are the big five arguments against astrology. You've probably heard them all before:

1. *Newspaper and magazine predictions are too general—they could mean anything.*
2. *How can the planets affect our lives when they're so far away?*
3. *Astrologers just make it up.*
4. *How can the future be the same for one in twelve people?*
5. *If astrology works, why aren't all astrologers millionaires?*

OK, get ready for the five big answers:

I write horoscope prediction columns for many magazines around the world, including *Cosmopolitan* and *New*

Woman. They are general predictions because media astrology is a general business. I only know your Star Sign, after all—I don't know your Rising Sign, or your Moon Sign, or anything about your midheaven—and these really matter.

However, some things really stand out. Because you're a Gemini, I know that contact with people from other countries, backgrounds or cultures has created radical changes in your view of the world since 1996. That is a general statement, based on the fact that Uranus, the planet of change, has recently been in the 9th House, which is your department of overseas travel, foreigners and your perception of the world.

I can't nail it down to specifics about your travel plans in my columns because I don't know if you are the kind of woman who has a jetsetter's budget, or if you're content to explore a different side of your own country for the moment. By the way, no astrologer knows this. That's why we can only predict your future in fairly general terms, talking about a broad concept like change via people from other countries.

It's a bit like weather forecasters. They can only ever tell you about possible showers over certain parts of your area. Because they have to take in such a large audience living all over the place, they have to make sweeping generalizations. They could probably tell you that at five minutes past one when you open your front door it's going to pour down with rain, but only if you get the forecaster over for a personal consultation!

It's the same with astrology. A personal horoscope consultation (based on the time, date and year of your birth) will be stunningly accurate, specific and detailed in the hands of a good astrologer. In the meantime, magazine and newspaper forecasts are pretty damn good. Not all the time. But most of the time. Want to hear some?

The Experiment Subject: Hillary Clinton (Scorpio)
The Event: Bill Clinton's affair with Monica Lewinsky goes public
The Date: August 1998

☆ **The Astrologer:** Elizabeth Potier
The Magazine: U.S. *Elle*
She Said: Scorpio—"Around the 21st, ask yourself 'Are others being dishonest or simply stupid?' Perhaps a little of both. Find your forgiveness zone and remember that sometimes happiness depends on how much you can overlook."

☆ **The Astrologer:** Marjorie Orr
The Magazine: UK *Saturday*
She Said: Scorpio—"There may be muddles and misunderstandings with family members

which make you panic on and off until August when you need to be firm but fair. Lay your cards on the table and insist everyone else does the same. June to September could be a cooling period with certain close mates. Saturn is pointing out flaws and inadequacies. In certain relationships this could mean a parting of the ways."

One of the things that makes a great astrology column is the smart advice, as well as the accuracy of the prediction. And that's basically what it's all about. By looking at the positions of the planets in the heavens, astrologers who know their stuff can give you time-honored advice, based on at least 500 years of testing and research by the stargazers who have gone before. They can give you insights so that you are free to make a more informed choice about your life. We call it predicting, but of course, it's only the fact that a column is printed at the beginning of the month that turns the words into predictions. Astrology's real function is to explain the present. To look at it in terms of opportunities not to be missed and painful experiences to be understood, or even avoided.

Even though you might accept that astrology works, how do you get your head around the fact that a distant planet like Pluto can possibly affect a woman down here on planet Earth?

There are many explanations of the "how it works" variety. Read *The Scientific Basis of Astrology,* by Percy Seymour, if you need to know more. Basically, what I do is just pick up a hefty book and chuck it at skeptics. They're quite heavy in hardback and make good ammunition. A skeptic, by the way, is usually someone who read the side of a Snoopy Star Sign coffee mug in 1973 and has based his entire argument on that.

Excuse me for getting a little obstreperous here. But after all, I do this for a living. And no, I don't make it up (neither does any other media astrologer, to my knowledge).

I know it might sound strange that just because you are a Gemini, you can be going through the same basic life experiences as one-twelfth of the population. Think of Star Signs as being similar to gender, though, and it doesn't look quite so weird. Women have repeated life patterns: we have the menstrual cycle to deal with, just because we were born female; we also know in advance when we're likely to experience menopause; and when we get pregnant we can usually predict the timed outcome of that too! Being born under the label "woman" means you'll go through life with a higher-pitched voice, among other things. At the end of the day, astrological labeling isn't that different. It's all cosmic number crunching, and knowing you're a Gemini or a Libra, or whatever, is no more mysterious than knowing you're a woman. Based on what astrologers know about these signs, they can also make predictions for you, or talk about general characteristics.

And, by the way, there is no such thing as a cusp. You really are either one sign or the other. Give your birth details to an astrologer and they can sort it all out for you.

This knowledge is enough to make astrologers—or their clients—wealthy. And quite a few of them are (though they don't talk about it much). However, in order to make millions from this business, you have to be born with the sort of birth horoscope that leans toward you being good with money or lucky with deals. If you were born with a tricky cash chart, you can time Jupiter trines to the 2nd House for all you are worth (sorry, I had to stick some astro-lingo in there!) and you're still not going to take Ivana Trump out to lunch.

Astrology works. It's so accurate that sometimes I believe what it tells me even when the evidence is going against it. In December 1996, *New Weekly* magazine in Australia asked me to predict Brad Pitt's year ahead.

They were carrying stories about his blissful romance with Gwyneth Paltrow at the time, and photographs of them in poolside full-frontal hugs. It wasn't easy to print this, but after looking at Brad's chart, I had to do it.

***New Weekly*, December 1996:** "Brad's relationship with Gwyneth Paltrow has been formed at a time when he is not 100 percent clear about what he wants or needs. It will be tested out in 1997, when one of them will have to deal with a cooling-off period."

In June 1997 they split up.

I wrote Emma Thompson's year-ahead prediction on her birthday.

***New Weekly*, April 1995:** "Emma's love life this year looks very complicated. She faces some difficult questions with husband Kenneth Branagh in April and June."

Six months later, they separated.

Good astrologers never, ever predict actual separation or divorce—firstly on the grounds that they wouldn't want to hear it, so why would you? And secondly on the grounds that it's impossible. Clairvoyants predict specific events. Astrologers can only predict general moods and trends. If you choose to do something major, like leave your husband, that's your business. We can only tell you the emotional weather at the time and hopefully guide your decision by supplying extra information and insight.

Finally, let's be real about this. It doesn't work with 100 percent accuracy all the time. This may be because astrologers are only human and, like doctors, they occasionally make a wrong diagnosis. It may also be because of the planet Uranus, which rules chaos theory, and consequently mucks everything up now and again—and Neptune, which rules confusion. Astrologers accept that Uranus and Neptune are part of the deal, and if we do that, we also have to live with the fact that our insights will sometimes be wrong, because that's what these planets stand for—chaos and confusion! The occasional wrong call may even be part of the greater pattern that makes most of it right.

For the most part, though, astrology will work for you if you let it, and it's like weather forecasting for the soul. Did you know that most magazine astrologers have to send in their columns over three months before the issue appears on the newsstands? In year-ahead predictions we are often working a whole 12 months into the future. Skeptics and some prejudiced scientists knock us, but we are prepared to go into print, and on the record, ahead of time—every time.

Here's Penny Thornton (former astrologer to Princess Diana) predicting Bill Clinton's year ahead in January 1998, in Australia's *Who Weekly* magazine: "He seems invulnerable to anything the cosmos can throw at him and will ride through 1998's holocausts. The scandals won't stop, but if he's emerged smelling like a rose before, he'll do it again."

My advice is to check astrology, test it and use it. It's there so you can understand what the hell is actually going on when things are bad, and so that you can energetically exploit life's more fabulous opportunities when they come your way.

TWO

What It *Really* Means to Be a Gemini Woman

OK. Let's start at the beginning and be straight about this. Here's what you're not—

Moody. Two-faced. Split personality.

A lot of rubbish gets written about your sign. This is because someone made it all up in about 1930 and it's just been recycled ever since. I've seen the most bizarre things about Gemini printed inside birthday cards ("You're intelligent"). Well, that's nice for your ego, but it has nothing to do with astrology—or what it really means to be a Gemini.

How does a sign get "given" characteristics anyway? It began with the first stargazers, who noticed that people born when the sun appeared to be passing through a certain zodiac constellation seemed to have traits in common. The pattern of stars that makes up Gemini the Twins could really be anything—a sponge cake, a postbox, a golden retriever. The fact that the ancients decided the stars joined together to make the shape of twins is significant, though.

You may not be a twin, but brothers and sisters are very important in your life. If you were an only child, or if you had a brother or sister who died, that is equally significant. The lack of a sibling will be just as important in forming your personality and shaping your life as a strong bond (or even a bad relationship) with a sister or brother would have been. By the way, if you're the only child in the family, you may have found a twin substitute. Either a man you have a platonic and close friendship with, or a woman who is practically the sister you never had. As a Gemini, your life and times will be profoundly influenced by this other character—your true or substitute sibling.

Geminis Kylie Minogue and Joan Collins are almost as well known for their famous sisters (Dannii Minogue and Jackie Collins) as they are for their own achievements. The Gemini writer Margaret Drabble and her sister, novelist A. S. Byatt, provide another famous example of this phenomenon.

Gemini Realities

- *You're about words—writing, talking, reading, sign language, the telephone, e-mail or fax.*
- *A real-life sibling, or a substitute sibling in your life, says a huge amount about your personality.*
- *You are typically known by another name than the one you were christened with (even a nickname), or you tend to make up your own names for other people, animals, or objects.*

"We are not amused."
Queen Victoria, born 24 May 1819

Natural Psychologists

Researcher and author Gunter Sachs *(The Astrology File)* studied over 231,000 university students to find out which signs of the zodiac were interested in what subjects. Geminis were significantly more interested in psychology than other signs. Your sign is much less likely to study pharmacy than psychology, for example. Human nature is your thing.

One thing you can't predict from your Gemini Star Sign is your career, though, so don't believe anything you've read about becoming a journalist, or a teacher or a secretary. What I can say about you is this much: you're curious about people, you enjoy knowing what makes people tick, and you prefer analyzing people's motives to analyzing bottles of chemicals.

Who Do You Get Along With?

It's wrong to say that you're most compatible with Libra or Aquarius—or that you don't get along with Sagittarius. You've probably read things like that everywhere, but in actual fact you need to have full horoscopes drawn up for you and your partner if you want to know the whole truth. A relationship or a marriage is extremely complicated, and so is astrology. That's why comparing something as basic as Star Signs gets you nowhere!

For the real story you need to see a professional astrologer:

- *Your Moon Sign will have to be compared to your man's chart to see how you'll feel about living together or starting a family. How would you deal with illness, miscarriage or moving house? Your Moon Signs describe if you're going to see life the same way and be there for each other emotionally and domestically.*
- *Your Venus Sign will have to be compared to your man's chart to see how romantic, erotic and loving*

your relationship's really going to be. If you want a long-term relationship or marriage where the passion never really fades, then you will need strong chemistry based on your Venus Signs.

- *Your Mercury Sign will have to be compared to his chart, too, to see if there will be communication problems. Will phone calls be easy for both of you, or will it never feel quite right? What about clear understanding and good listening skills? Mercury Signs matter.*
- *Your Mars Sign will have to be compared to his chart to see how both of you are going to handle irritation, anger or stress as a couple. Mars also has an influence on sexual tension, and sex in general. Will you drive each other mad, or can you deal with anger constructively?*

What I can say about chemistry and compatibility is this. What you're actually looking for, in terms of recognizing something in a man which is also part of you, lies in chapter six ("Profile of Your Soulmate"). You know that "click" feeling you get with certain lovers? Part of it comes from identifying certain bits of a bloke's heart, soul or brain that strongly resonate with bits of you. Is your soulmate a star, a thinker, a rock or a caretaker? Skip to page 68 right away to find out. But if you're really serious about long-term chemistry and compatibility, get both your charts compared. The Internet has several sites where you can order these, and other kinds of charts. I recommend The Astrology Shop online at www.astrology.co.uk (it has special sections for the UK, USA and Australia) as a good starting point.

THREE

Surfing the Stars— How to Make the Most of the 21st Century

In this section, you'll see where the major breakthroughs and plus factors are over the next seven years. If you sit back and do nothing, it's possible that you'll get what you want without trying. However, if you are looking for something major, be proactive. Don't just let fate take you for a ride—double your luck by catching the wave and then getting everything you can from it while it's there. In other words, if your social life is set to take off during Easter 2000, that's the time to consciously follow up every opportunity. Especially if it involves friends who can lend you their beachside mansions, and parties with piña colada on tap.

I could give you all sorts of predictions for the 21st century—job traumas, money hassles, love-life dramas or health problems. After ten years as an astrologer, though, I have come to believe that the most useful thing you can hear is the good stuff. (By the way, I just made all that bad stuff up.) What's on offer to you in this new century? Where's the good news coming from? That's what astrology is all about. Consequently I'm not going to utter any dire warnings or doom and gloom predictions. What I want to do in this section is show you how good life could be—and where the growth spurts are going to come from. The rest is up to you.

DATELINE: MARCH AND APRIL 2000, 2001, 2003, 2006, 2007

Catch the Wave: Group Energy, Fantastic Friendships

Look at the possibilities with a group, team, club or other organizations in March and April of 2000, 2001, 2003, 2006 and 2007. These are amazing periods in your life when you could get involved with a band that takes the music world by storm, or an evening class in African voodoo. The idea is to focus on group energy. People power. Your love life is all very well, and your family is another situation entirely. But what about sharing in common goals with people, no matter if you're chasing a sports trophy together, taking a group holiday, or doing the 40 Hour Famine? These months are good times to make the first move and join something—anything. Closer to home, you may find that it is a tight circle of friends—maybe a gang of four—which changes your life for the better.

Friends in general are in the spotlight in these March–April periods. You'll come closer to understanding what true friendship is during these times. Friendship with men, for example, can exist in a no-sex, no-ties, no-complications way. It's unconditional fun, unconditional trust and mutual appreciation. With women, you can really have more fun in your life, more meaning in your world, and a few practical pay-offs as well. Friends could even change your life in a few of the years mentioned. You'll meet new friends who seem like they've been around forever, and get a lot more from your old friends as well.

Five fantasies for March–April 2000, 2001, 2003, 2006, 2007

1. *You form an all-girl band and end up winning a record deal.*
2. *Your new best friend is a multimillionaire—he puts you in his will.*
3. *Your yoga group changes your health, and your entire life.*
4. *An old friend from childhood reappears and offers you a hot job.*
5. *On your birthday, your friends organize a surprise party for 300.*

Now, make up your own fantasies . . .

To give you an idea of what is possible for you, think about Jerry Seinfeld. He went through this same cycle from 1989 to 1992, when the Seinfeld team of friends first got together. As a solo stand-up comedian, he discovered his route to success through group energy. You, too, might get a new angle on your career by getting together with a bunch of like-minded people. Or, you could join a gym, get selected for a soccer team, enroll in Japanese classes or any other activity where people from different backgrounds unite together for a common goal—and new friends. Gemini Courteney Cox is having the same cycle as you right now. Funnily enough, the hit show she stars in is (of course) called *Friends*.

The other interesting thing about this cycle is that your friends will show you who you are. What you love about them is also inside your own personality. Friends in these months could even hold up a mirror for your own life. The issues that they face may be exactly the same as your own, but disguised! Through friends and groups, you will get to know yourself better at these times. You will very much identify with being part of a certain circle of friends in these periods, or part of a specific group.

Through work, you may find yourself naturally being pushed into a tight team environment. If you can balance your own needs with those of the group, you will find that March–April of the key years mentioned above turns out to be an incredibly productive period. You'll learn that you can be yourself and still be with other people and that, in a funny kind of way, you wouldn't take such a starring role unless you were part of this same group. You need each other, and feed off each other.

In a few words: Friends and groups will make life seem better, happier, more fulfilling.
Look for: Old friends to look up, new friends on the fringes, advertisements for clubs, classes or societies.
If you do nothing: You'll still feel as if friends can matter more than lovers.
If you push things: A group of friends could completely change your life.

DATELINE: SEPTEMBER AND OCTOBER 2000, 2002, 2005, 2006, 2007

Catch the Wave: Creativity, Love, Children

If you are very lucky, you will find wonderful things happening with kids, lovers and creative interests all in the same month. It's more likely that just one area of your life will come through at a time, though. So September–October may be the period you discover creative gambling at the casino, or the fine art of beach volleyball (with flair). Many Geminis are destined to produce novels, paintings, music or some other kind of "brainchild" in these periods. The self-expression you can find will be amazing, as the combined forces of Uranus, Neptune and Pluto are pushing this side of you.

Sport may become more artful, more like entertainment. And decorating your home, or putting special effort into a work project, could become your vehicle for projecting your personality, and showing the world who you are and what you can do. A person you know may act as your muse, or something else could totally inspire you. Don't be surprised if you develop a passion for writing short stories, or trying your hand at dressmaking!

Five fantasies for September–October 2000, 2002, 2005, 2006, 2007

1. *You sew some outfits for yourself and end up with your own Paris label.*
2. *You adopt young twin girls who turn out to be talented violinists.*
3. *You meet the love of your life at the moment you least expect it.*
4. *You switch sexual preferences and finally marry—at Mardi Gras.*

5. You get a handycam for Christmas and shoot an Oscar-winning film.

Now, make up your own fantasies . . .

The kind of love you find in these periods is also quite creative. The sex will be more expressive, for example, and you will feel much more inclined to do something special, or memorable, or stylishly romantic. If you are single, your chances of finding new love are much higher during these September–October cycles. But will it last? For the answer to this, you'll need to wait until November–December, which is when your commitment cycle is in focus. By Christmas, you'll always know where you stand.

You can have lots of fun in the September–October period of the years listed above. You can take a more playful approach toward love. If you don't particularly want commitments, and sex is too complicated, you could develop a hands-off flirtation with someone and enjoy every minute of it.

Wonderful and rewarding connections with children may be a feature of the time frames listed above. On an obvious level, you could get pregnant then, or give birth, or celebrate a breakthrough with your existing son or daughter. You might adopt a child, become a godparent or aunt, or be asked to baby-sit, or just spend more time with other people's children. It should be an exciting and inspiring time for you.

In a few words: Target children, great ideas, fun, love and creativity for maximum effects.
Look for: A project, hobby or interest which truly allows you to express yourself fully.
If you do nothing: You could get lucky in love, or find yourself unexpectedly pregnant.
If you push things: You could become a mother, meet your soulmate, or have a hit single.

FOUR

Dates for Your Diary

Jupiter, Saturn, Uranus, Neptune and Pluto are the power points of astrology. Between the dates below, you will plug into these power points as the planets make major patterns in your horoscope. A significant event may occur on just one day in the ten-day time spans below. Or you may find something gathers speed over the course of a week or more. You don't have to take Jupiter's opportunities or open yourself up to Uranus's radical changes. But if you feel something going on at these times and you can't quite get it straight in your head, this section may spell it out and help you to focus. These are really important power points in your year, so watch out for them.

Some power points repeat every year. The situation may be different each time, but the issues underneath will be exactly the same. This is why I've left space for your own notes underneath some sections. When you encounter the same Pluto power point, for example, go back to your notes from previous years. This is probably the best thing you can do for yourself in handling the future! By learning from other power point times in the past, you will know a little of what to expect, and you will also know what you did right or wrong last time.

2000

20–30 January

Neptune Power Point

The Focus: People, places and ideas which broaden your horizon in every kind of way.

The Issue: Traveling in the mind, or moving away from your usual base and headspace.

Your Choice: Swapping perspectives or putting yourself in others' shoes educates you.

Notes: This power point will repeat every year until 2005. Take notes on the following lines:

1–11 February

Uranus Power Point

The Focus: Your country, your world, your universe and your perspective on where you are.

The Issues: Honesty. Differences and individuality. Dealing with change. Tolerance.

Your Choice: Be proud of what you believe and accept that others are proud of their beliefs too.

Notes: This power point will repeat every year until 2003. Take notes here:

____

____

____

4–14 May

Jupiter Power Point

The Focus: Life behind the scenes. Secret or confidential matters. The background stuff.

The Issues: Opportunities. Recognition. Confidence. Total optimism.

Your Choice: You can shine now, and take the smallest opportunity and open it up.

Remember: This power point will not happen again for 12 years.

6–16 May

Saturn Power Point

The Focus: What you do in your own time. Matters that you can't really share around.

The Issues: Patience. Believing in yourself. Taking a reality check. Dealing with heavy stuff.

Your Choice: Express yourself, lead the way, or take the spotlight—and take the burden.

Remember: This power point will not happen again for 29 years.

29 November–9 December

Pluto Power Point

The Focus: Situations that revolve around Me and You, or even Me versus You.

The Issues: Transformation. Power. Control. Real depth. Anything you think of as a taboo.

Your Choice: You are who you are, so express it. Change things or find your own power.

Notes: This power point will repeat every year until 2005. Take notes here:

____

____

____

2001

21–31 January

Neptune Power Point

The Focus: Whatever gives you the big picture in terms of people, places, ideas or plans.

The Issue: Floating onto another level to look at what is real—and unreal—about it all.

Your Choice: Healthy self-esteem makes it possible to put your ego second.

Notes: This power point will repeat every year until 2005. Take notes here:

____

____

____

4–14 February

Uranus Power Point

The Focus: Where you're traveling, in terms of a world map or your own attitudes.

The Issue: Allowing lightning bolts to jolt you awake and show you what's true for you.

Your Choice: Why stick to old rules, attitudes or setups if they no longer work for now?

Notes: This power point will repeat every year until 2003. Take notes here:

20–30 May
Saturn Power Point

The Focus: You, basically. Your image, your appearance and how you project yourself.

The Issue: How do you take yourself more seriously without going overboard about it?

Your Choice: By taking certain realities about yourself on board you'll make headway.

Notes: This power point will repeat next year—it's an ongoing theme. Take notes here:

9–19 June
Jupiter Power Point

The Focus: Your outer packaging, from your clothes to your hair. Your public persona.

The Issues: Luck—is it fate, or do you make it happen? Positive thinking. Opportunities.

Your Choice: Express yourself on the outside, and radiate confidence to feel confidence.

Remember: This power point will not happen again for 12 years.

2–12 December

Pluto Power Point

The Focus: Husbands, de facto partners, lovers, exes, rivals, enemies or business partners.

The Issues: Going more deeply into things; realizing that change is an intense business.

Your Choice: Confidence means never being content to live life on the surface.

Notes: This power point will repeat every year until 2005. Take notes here:

____

____

____

____

____

2002

20 January–2 February

Neptune Power Point

The Focus: Any place, person, idea or setup that stretches you mentally and spiritually.

The Issue: Feeling for others as you would feel for yourself, no matter what the situation.

Your Choice: Enlightened beings only get that way through kindness.

Notes: This power point will repeat every year until 2005. Take notes here:

____

____

____

____

8–18 February

Uranus Power Point

The Focus: What you believe to be true about yourself, the world you live in and other people.

The Issues: Life (and people) can be unpredictable, and a wake-up and a shake-up amount to the same thing.

Your Choice: True freedom and a greater sense of being alive come with tolerance.

Notes: This power point will repeat next year. Take notes here:

4–14 June

Saturn Power Point

The Focus: The way you package yourself to the world, and the way you advertise yourself.

The Issues: Thinking things through that you cannot change. Being a realist. Finding patience.

Your Choice: There's something noble about doing all the right things this month.

Remember: This power point happened last year, so check your notes on page 29.

15–25 July

Jupiter Power Point

The Focus: Money, possessions, houses and apartments. Your personal set of values.

The Issues: Seeing the positive, pursuing the possibilities, not the impossibilities.

Your Choice: You can take something small and do a whole lot more with it.

Remember: This power point will not happen again for 12 years.

4–14 December

Pluto Power Point

The Focus: The other person. Which could be your partner, an ex-partner or even an enemy.

The Issue: Where is your power base or sense of control?

Your Choice: You, or a setup around you, could be the grub that turns into a butterfly.

Notes: This power point will repeat every year until 2005. Take notes here:

____

____

2003

25 January–4 February

Neptune Power Point

The Focus: Books, the Internet, mentors, trips away or what educates you.

The Issue: Knowing that it's sometimes in your self-interest to put yourself second.

Your Choice: Spiritual, religious, psychic or cosmic people could show you a lot now.

Notes: This power point will repeat every year until 2005. Take notes here:

____

____

12–22 February
Uranus Power Point

The Focus: The ideas you grew up with, versus a brand new way of looking at your world.

The Issues: Living life in an honest, exciting, completely free way, despite the uncertainty.

Your Choice: Your confidence and sense of self fuses with your ability to accept change.

Remember: After three years of this cycle, you can now say goodbye to it—what did you learn?

17–27 August
Jupiter Power Point

The Focus: Communication. Good ideas. Brainwaves. Short trips away. Words.

The Issue: Looking for the possibilities, the "yes" answers, the green lights and the luck.

Your Choice: If you want to shine, believe in yourself and then wait for the words to come.
Remember: This power point will not happen again for 12 years.

6–16 December
Pluto Power Point

The Focus: Relationships, partnerships, soulmate connections (positive or negative).
The Issue: The one thing you can't talk about, or even face, is the biggest factor now.
Your Choice: By examining a taboo or off-limits topic, you open the way to change.
Notes: This power point will repeat every year until 2005. Take notes here:

____

____

(There is no Saturn Power Point this year.)

2004
28 January–7 February
Neptune Power Point

The Focus: Other accents, other places, other perspectives. Bigger and broader horizons.

The Issue: What is the difference between a meaningful sacrifice and martyring yourself?

Your Choice: Put yourself in somebody else's shoes—no matter what their taste in footwear.

Notes: This power point will repeat next year. Take notes here:

16–26 February

Uranus Power Point

The Focus: Success and achievement, and what they mean now. Your direction in life.

The Issues: Being open to a whole new order. Understanding what freedom actually means.

Your Choice: Do things differently, break some of your own rules and achieve a breakthrough.

Notes: This power point will repeat next year. Take notes here:

3–13 July
Saturn Power Point

The Focus: What you own, earn or owe. Cash, houses, cars, apartments, precious possessions.

The Issues: Accepting life as it is, not as you would like it to be. Hanging in there.

Your Choice: There's a kind of glory in being open to tough learning experiences.

Remember: This power point will not happen again for 29 years.

17–27 September
Jupiter Power Point

The Focus: Your house. Your family. Your apartment. Your roommates. Your roots or origins.

The Issue: Your sense of self (and identity) will be bound up with the home front.

Your Choice: Something could really improve or grow here, but it all begins with total optimism.

Remember: This power point will not happen again for 12 years.

9–19 December
Pluto Power Point

The Focus: Who you marry or live with. Who you love. A business partner. An enemy.

The Issues: Dealing with intensity in yourself or others. And how does power operate?

Your Choice: Before you change a setup, you have to change yourself.

Notes: This power point will repeat next year. Take notes here:

____

____

____

____

2005

30 January–9 February

Neptune Power Point

The Focus: People who are not like you, or people who come from different backgrounds or places.

The Issue: Blurring the boundaries means you see what Buddha saw—that we are all one.

Your Choice: Feeling proud of yourself begins with your choice to sympathize or empathize with others.

Remember: Your notes from Neptune power points in previous years could be useful now.

20 February–2 March

Uranus Power Point

The Focus: Where you are going in terms of your ambitions, goals or sense of mission.

The Issues: Radical change. Independence in yourself or another. Being true to yourself.

Your Choice: You know who you are, and career matters or other goals will reveal it.

Remember: Your notes from 2004 could be useful now.

19–29 July

Saturn Power Point

The Focus: Communication of all kinds. Connections and ideas. Contacts or trips.

The Issues: Accepting what you cannot change. Being able to take a few basic realities.

Your Choice: If something about your life is a serious matter, then take it seriously.

Remember: This power point will happen again next year!

16–26 October

Jupiter Power Point

The Focus: A child or baby in your world. Love, sex and romance. Or your creativity.

The Issue: If you think you can make it happen, then you probably can make it happen.

Your Choice: Recognize a blessing when you see it, no matter what form it takes.

Remember: Read "Catch the Wave: Creativity, Love, Children," on page 20, too.

11–21 December

Pluto Power Point

The Focus: The other person. But as always, the other person is also a reflection of you.

The Issue: A natural cycle is unfolding—like a plant growing, dying and producing seeds.

Your Choice: Resurrect something—yourself, another person, an attitude, a setup.

Remember: Your notes from Pluto power points in previous years could be useful now.

FIVE

Your Venus Sign—
Is This the Real You?

Not knowing your Venus Sign is like not knowing that you're a Gemini. It's just as important. Most of the time, it's actually different from your Star Sign—you might be a Gemini with a Cancer Venus Sign or a Taurus Venus Sign. Women often tell me that they feel their Venus Sign is really "them." Their Star Sign is in there too, but it's the Venus Sign that's really accurate.

It's not surprising, really. Venus is a female planet. When you fall in love, buy clothes, put on perfume or hang out with your girlfriends, you tend to live out the personality qualities of your Venus Sign. If you go to parties and people try to guess if you're an Aries or a Taurus or whatever (how annoying!) they might get your Venus Sign, not your Star Sign.

To find out your Venus Sign, look up your day and year of birth in the tables on the following pages. These show the change-over dates, so start with the month on the left-hand side and then work across to find which sign Venus was in when you were born. For example, if you were born on 5 January 1960, your Venus Sign is Sagittarius, but if you were born on 28 January of that year, then your Venus Sign is Capricorn.

If your birthday falls outside the years shown in these tables, check out www.astro.com on the Internet—it'll give you a free rundown of all your planets.

Don't worry if your Venus Sign is the same as your Star Sign—in other words, you happen to have a Gemini Venus Sign, too. It just makes you a classic double Gemini! In most cases, though, you're about to discover a whole new side of yourself . . .

1949

MTH	DAY	SIGN
JAN	1	SAG
JAN	13	CAP
FEB	6	AQU
MAR	2	PIS
MAR	26	ARI
APR	19	TAU
MAY	14	GEM
JUN	7	CAN
JUL	1	LEO
JUL	26	VIR
AUG	20	LIB
SEP	14	SCO
OCT	10	SAG
NOV	6	CAP
DEC	6	AQU

1950

MTH	DAY	SIGN
JAN	1	AQU
APR	6	PIS
MAY	5	ARI
JUN	1	TAU
JUN	27	GEM
JUL	22	CAN
AUG	16	LEO
SEP	10	VIR
OCT	4	LIB
OCT	28	SCO
NOV	21	SAG
DEC	14	CAP

1951

MTH	DAY	SIGN
JAN	1	CAP
JAN	7	AQU
JAN	31	PIS
FEB	24	ARI
MAR	21	TAU
APR	15	GEM
MAY	11	CAN
JUN	7	LEO
JUL	8	VIR
NOV	9	LIB
DEC	8	SCO

1952

MTH	DAY	SIGN
JAN	1	SCO
JAN	2	SAG
JAN	27	CAP
FEB	21	AQU
MAR	16	AQU
APR	9	ARI
MAY	4	TAU
MAY	28	GEM
JUN	22	CAN
JUL	16	LEO
AUG	9	VIR
SEP	3	LIB
SEP	27	SCO
OCT	22	SAG
NOV	15	CAP
DEC	10	AQU

1953

MTH	DAY	SIGN
JAN	1	AQU
JAN	5	PIS
FEB	2	ARI
MAR	14	TAU
MAR	31	ARI
JUN	5	TAU
JUL	7	GEM
AUG	4	CAN
AUG	30	LEO
SEP	24	VIR
OCT	18	LIB
NOV	11	SCO
DEC	5	SAG
DEC	29	CAP

1954

MTH	DAY	SIGN
JAN	1	CAP
JAN	22	AQU
FEB	15	PIS
MAR	11	ARI
APR	4	TAU
APR	28	GEM
MAY	23	CAN
JUN	17	LEO
JUL	13	VIR
AUG	9	LIB
SEP	6	SCO
OCT	23	SAG
OCT	27	SCO

1955

MTH	DAY	SIGN
JAN	1	SCO
JAN	6	SAG
FEB	6	CAP
MAR	4	AQU
MAR	30	PIS
APR	24	ARI
MAY	19	TAU
JUN	13	GEM
JUL	8	CAN
AUG	1	LEO
AUG	25	VIR
SEP	18	LIB
OCT	13	SCO
NOV	6	SAG
NOV	30	CAP
DEC	24	AQU

1956

MTH	DAY	SIGN
JAN	1	AQU
JAN	17	PIS
FEB	11	ARI
MAR	7	TAU
APR	4	GEM
MAY	8	CAN
JUN	23	GEM
AUG	4	CAN
SEP	8	LEO
OCT	6	VIR
OCT	31	LIB
NOV	25	SCO
DEC	19	SAG

1957

MTH	DAY	SIGN
JAN	1	SAG
JAN	12	CAP
FEB	5	AQU
MAR	1	PIS
MAR	25	ARI
APR	19	TAU
MAY	13	GEM
JUN	6	CAN
JUL	1	LEO
JUL	26	VIR
AUG	20	LIB
SEP	14	SCO
OCT	10	SAG
NOV	5	CAP
DEC	6	AQU

1958

MTH	DAY	SIGN
JAN	1	AQU
APR	6	PIS
MAY	5	ARI
JUN	1	TAU
JUN	26	GEM
JUL	22	CAN
AUG	16	LEO
SEP	9	VIR
OCT	3	LIB
OCT	27	SCO
NOV	20	SAG
DEC	14	CAP

1959

MTH	DAY	SIGN
JAN	1	CAP
JAN	7	AQU
JAN	31	PIS
FEB	24	ARI
MAR	20	TAU
APR	14	GEM
MAY	10	CAN
JUN	6	LEO
JUL	8	VIR
SEP	20	LEO
SEP	25	VIR
NOV	9	LIB
DEC	7	SCO

1960

MTH	DAY	SIGN
JAN	1	SCO
JAN	2	SAG
JAN	27	CAP
FEB	20	AQU
MAR	16	PIS
APR	9	ARI
MAY	3	TAU
MAY	28	GEM
JUN	21	CAN
JUL	16	LEO
AUG	9	VIR
SEP	2	LIB
SEP	27	SCO
OCT	21	SAG
NOV	15	CAP
DEC	10	AQU

1961

MTH	DAY	SIGN
JAN	1	AQU
JAN	5	PIS
FEB	2	ARI
JUN	5	TAU
JUL	7	GEM
AUG	3	CAN
AUG	29	LEO
SEP	23	VIR
OCT	18	LIB
NOV	11	SCO
DEC	5	SAG
DEC	29	CAP

1962

MTH	DAY	SIGN
JAN	1	CAP
JAN	21	AQU
FEB	14	PIS
MAR	10	ARI
APR	3	TAU
APR	28	GEM
MAY	23	CAN
JUN	17	LEO
JUL	12	VIR
AUG	8	LIB
SEP	7	SCO

1963

MTH	DAY	SIGN
JAN	1	SCO
JAN	6	SAG
FEB	5	CAP
MAR	4	AQU
MAR	30	PIS
APR	24	ARI
MAY	19	TAU
JUN	12	GEM
JUL	7	CAN
JUL	31	LEO
AUG	25	VIR
SEP	18	LIB
OCT	12	SCO
NOV	5	SAG
NOV	29	CAP
DEC	23	AQU

1964

MTH	DAY	SIGN
JAN	1	AQU
JAN	17	PIS
FEB	10	ARI
MAR	7	TAU
APR	4	GEM
MAY	9	CAN
JUN	17	GEM
AUG	5	CAN
SEP	8	LEO
OCT	5	VIR
OCT	31	LIB
NOV	25	SCO
DEC	19	SAG

1965

MTH	DAY	SIGN
JAN	1	SAG
JAN	12	CAP
FEB	5	AQU
MAR	1	PIS
MAR	25	ARI
APR	18	TAU
MAY	12	GEM
JUN	6	CAN
JUN	30	LEO
JUL	25	VIR
AUG	19	LIB
SEP	13	SCO
OCT	9	SAG
NOV	5	CAP
DEC	7	AQU

1966

MTH	DAY	SIGN
JAN	1	AQU
FEB	6	CAP
FEB	25	AQU
APR	6	PIS
MAY	5	ARI
MAY	31	TAU
JUN	26	GEM
JUL	21	CAN
AUG	15	LEO
SEP	8	VIR
OCT	3	LIB
OCT	27	SCO
NOV	20	SAG
DEC	13	CAP

1967

MTH	DAY	SIGN
JAN	1	CAP
JAN	6	AQU
JAN	30	PIS
FEB	23	ARI
MAR	20	TAU
APR	14	GEM
MAY	10	CAN
JUN	6	LEO
JUL	8	VIR
SEP	9	LEO
OCT	1	VIR
NOV	9	LIB
DEC	7	SCO

1968

MTH	DAY	SIGN
JAN	1	SAG
JAN	26	CAP
FEB	20	AQU
MAR	15	PIS
APR	8	ARI
MAY	3	TAU
MAY	27	GEM
JUN	21	CAN
JUL	15	LEO
AUG	8	VIR
SEP	2	LIB
SEP	26	SCO
OCT	21	SAG
NOV	14	CAP
DEC	9	AQU

1969

MTH	DAY	SIGN
JAN	1	AQU
JAN	4	PIS
FEB	2	ARI
JUN	6	TAU
JUL	6	GEM
AUG	3	CAN
SEP	23	VIR
OCT	17	LIB
NOV	10	SCO
DEC	4	SAG
DEC	28	CAP

1970

MTH	DAY	SIGN
JAN	1	CAP
JAN	21	AQU
FEB	14	PIS
MAR	10	ARI
APR	3	TAU
APR	27	GEM
MAY	22	CAN
JUN	16	LEO
JUL	12	VIR
AUG	8	LIB
SEP	7	SCO

1971

MTH	DAY	SIGN
JAN	1	SCO
JAN	7	SAG
FEB	5	CAP
MAR	4	AQU
MAR	29	PIS
APR	23	ARI
MAY	18	TAU
JUN	12	GEM
JUL	6	CAN
JUL	31	LEO
AUG	24	VIR
SEP	17	LIB
OCT	11	SCO
NOV	5	SAG
NOV	29	CAP
DEC	23	AQU

1972

MTH	DAY	SIGN
JAN	1	AQU
JAN	16	PIS
FEB	10	ARI
MAR	7	TAU
APR	3	GEM
MAY	10	CAN
JUN	11	GEM
AUG	6	CAN
SEP	7	LEO
OCT	5	VIR
OCT	30	LIB
NOV	24	SCO
DEC	18	SAG

1973

MTH	DAY	SIGN
JAN	1	SAG
JAN	11	CAP
FEB	4	AQU
FEB	28	PIS
MAR	24	ARI
APR	18	TAU
MAY	12	GEM
JUN	5	CAN
JUN	30	LEO
JUL	25	VIR
AUG	19	LIB
SEP	13	SCO
OCT	9	SAG
NOV	5	CAP
DEC	7	AQU

1974

MTH	DAY	SIGN
JAN	1	AQU
JAN	29	CAP
FEB	28	AQU
APR	6	PIS
MAY	4	ARI
MAY	31	TAU
JUN	25	GEM
JUL	21	CAN
AUG	14	LEO
SEP	8	VIR
OCT	2	LIB
OCT	26	SCO
NOV	19	SAG
DEC	13	CAP

1975

MTH	DAY	SIGN
JAN	1	CAP
JAN	6	AQU
JAN	30	PIS
FEB	23	ARI
MAR	19	TAU
APR	13	GEM
MAY	9	CAN
JUN	6	LEO
JUL	9	VIR
SEP	2	LEO
OCT	4	VIR
NOV	9	LIB
DEC	7	SCO

1976

MTH	DAY	SIGN
JAN	1	SAG
JAN	25	CAP
FEB	19	AQU
MAR	14	PIS
APR	7	ARI
MAY	2	TAU
MAY	27	GEM
JUN	20	CAN
JUL	14	LEO
AUG	7	VIR
SEP	1	LIB
SEP	25	SCO
OCT	20	SAG
NOV	14	CAP
DEC	9	AQU

1977

MTH	DAY	SIGN
JAN	1	AQU
JAN	4	PIS
FEB	2	ARI
JUN	6	TAU
JUL	6	GEM
AUG	2	CAN
AUG	28	LEO
SEP	22	VIR
OCT	17	LIB
NOV	10	SCO
DEC	4	SAG
DEC	27	CAP

1978

MTH	DAY	SIGN
JAN	1	CAP
JAN	20	AQU
FEB	13	PIS
MAR	9	ARI
APR	2	TAU
APR	27	GEM
MAY	22	CAN
JUN	16	LEO
JUL	12	VIR
AUG	8	LIB
SEP	7	SCO

1979

MTH	DAY	SIGN
JAN	1	SCO
JAN	7	SAG
FEB	5	CAP
MAR	3	AQU
MAR	29	PIS
APR	23	ARI
MAY	18	TAU
JUN	11	GEM
JUL	6	CAN
JUL	30	LEO
AUG	24	VIR
SEP	17	LIB
OCT	11	SCO
NOV	4	SAG
NOV	28	CAP
DEC	22	AQU

1980

MTH	DAY	SIGN
JAN	1	AQU
JAN	16	PIS
FEB	9	ARI
MAR	6	TAU
APR	3	GEM
MAY	12	CAN
JUN	5	GEM
AUG	6	CAN
SEP	7	LEO
OCT	4	VIR
OCT	30	LIB
NOV	24	SCO
DEC	18	SAG

1981

MTH	DAY	SIGN
JAN	1	SAG
JAN	11	CAP
FEB	4	AQU
FEB	28	PIS
MAR	24	ARI
APR	17	TAU
MAY	11	GEM
JUN	5	CAN
JUN	29	LEO
JUL	24	VIR
AUG	18	LIB
SEP	12	SCO
OCT	9	SAG
NOV	5	CAP
DEC	8	AQU

1982

MTH	DAY	SIGN
JAN	1	AQU
JAN	23	CAP
MAR	2	AQU
APR	6	PIS
MAY	4	ARI
MAY	30	TAU
JUN	25	GEM
JUL	20	CAN
AUG	14	LEO
SEP	7	VIR
OCT	2	LIB
OCT	26	SCO
NOV	18	SAG
DEC	12	CAP

1983

MTH	DAY	SIGN
JAN	1	CAP
JAN	5	AQU
JAN	29	PIS
FEB	22	ARI
MAR	19	TAU
APR	13	GEM
MAY	9	CAN
JUN	6	LEO
JUL	10	VIR
AUG	27	LEO
OCT	5	VIR
NOV	9	LIB
DEC	6	SCO

1984

MTH	DAY	SIGN
JAN	1	SAG
JAN	25	CAP
FEB	19	AQU
MAR	14	PIS
APR	7	ARI
MAY	2	TAU
MAY	26	GEM
JUN	20	CAN
JUL	14	LEO
AUG	7	VIR
SEP	1	LIB
SEP	25	SCO
OCT	20	SAG
NOV	13	CAP
DEC	9	AQU

Venus in Aries

You don't play games, and you don't hang around. If you want to dance someone into bed, you will. If you want to punch someone in the nose, you will. Your style is playful, loud, energetic and oomphy. You're not exactly subtle (how many people have told you that?) but life is too short—and anyway, who cares? It's true that you need a reasonable amount of fire, spark or tension to remain interested in someone. You may be an extreme Venus in Aries type, too, in which case fighting will be part of a relationship pattern. If things settle down and become predictable, you tend to feel uncomfortable. You're not really into cozy coupledom, it's far too boring. The only bigger turnoff is probably wimpy love—the kind that hides behind corners and spends ages making itself obvious. You are out there and up there, and some people love it, and some people loathe it. You like instant results, fast journeys, hot music, loud kissing. You're always six years old, somehow.

What's in your bedroom? Boots or sneakers, thrown on the floor. Red lipstick.
Get his horoscope done! If he's got planets in Aries, Leo or Sagittarius—Ping!
Get him into bed: Pretend to arm-wrestle him or

pillow-fight him. Yell "Get out!" and shove him, like Elaine in *Seinfeld*.

Women like you: Chrissie Hynde, Sarah Ferguson, Vivienne Westwood, Lucy from *Peanuts*, Xena the Warrior Princess.

Venus in Taurus

You know what's valuable. It may be that antique amethyst ring you bought for a song at a country auction, or the donation you made to the Red Cross last year. You're financially secure, have an excellent idea of market values, or a strong sense of ethics which goes beyond mere capitalist fluff! You have a good eye for what's beautiful and either appreciate others' artistic talents or have a few yourself. You love the touch of human skin, and heaven is an hour-long massage. You love wool, cotton, velvet. Natural smells and substances. Real flowers, not plastic ones. Your sensuality is highly developed. You love those indulgence days they offer at day spas with champagne, facials and scalp massages thrown in. Money is an issue for you, nonetheless. Luckily you're a born businesswoman or do-it-yourself accountant. Even if you give money to charity, you still know what a loaf of bread costs. Once you find out what you like in life, you stick to it quite stubbornly.

What's in your bedroom? One beautiful, valuable object. CDs. Massage oil.

Get his horoscope done! If he's got planets in Taurus, Capricorn or Virgo—Great!

Get him into bed: Rub his neck or shoulders, let him feel your wool or velvet jacket.

Women like you: Paloma Picasso, Barbra Streisand, Enya, Joanna Lumley, Her Majesty the Queen, Janet Jackson, Cher.

You're a Gemini with Venus in Taurus
Did you know that you will attract friends and/or lovers born under the signs of Taurus, Virgo and Capricorn?

Venus in Gemini

This side of you is funny and clever. Witty and well informed. You make the people around you smile, or just laugh, on a daily basis. You don't find it hard to network or make connections—it comes naturally to you, and you enjoy it. You swap business cards, e-mail addresses and phone numbers. You always know what's going on, and who said what to whom (and why). When life becomes too boring, heavy or embarrassing you know how to break it up with exactly the right comment, and people rely on you to do so. Friends, family or lovers make up nicknames for you, or you make up nicknames for them. You read the gossip columns—hell, you could write them. You always put the best comments on people's birthday cards. In your prime, you have run up phone bills bigger than your monthly food budget. You can't stand being bored. You can't cope with bimbos, or himbos. You're brainy and funny, and that's how you get to people. Works every time.

What's in your bedroom? Books, magazines, newspapers, telephone, notepad, pens.
Get his horoscope done! If he's got planets in Gemini, Libra or Aquarius—Ping!
Get him into bed: Be smarter than every other woman in the room. Be wittier, too.
Women like you: Candice Bergen, Victoria Wood, Nora Ephron (director of *Sleepless in Seattle* and *You've Got Mail*).

You're a Gemini with Venus in Gemini
Did you know that your strongest friendships and relationships will be with people whose Star Signs or Venus Signs are Aries, Leo, Gemini, Aquarius or Libra?

Venus in Cancer

You're a sweetie, but then you think other people are, too. You completely and genuinely care for people, and although you're not a saint, the time and energy you've thrown other people's way qualifies you for minor guru status. You can go too far (you know you can) and not everyone likes emotion or nurturing dripped over them. You make an excellent friend, lover or relative, however. You make people tea, offer them the comfy chair, ask them what's wrong, and give them second helpings of whatever they like. Your other great talent is making your house or apartment really feel like a home. It's not just your attention to domestic detail, design, color or atmosphere. It's because you believe your home is a place to pull people into—a kind of modern-day sanctuary, in fact. You love a family feel. If you can't get it from your own family, you assemble friends around you or create your own family later on. You need a clan around you. You need them, and they need you.

What's in your bedroom? Childhood things, gifts from people you love, photographs.

Get his horoscope done! If he's got planets in Cancer, Scorpio or Pisces—Ping!

Get him into bed: Cluck over him a bit, cuddle him, show cleavage or cook soup.

Women like you: Delia Smith, Princess Diana, Hazel Hawke, Mary Poppins, Kaye Webb (founder of Puffin children's books).

You're a Gemini with Venus in Cancer
Did you know that some of your closest friends or partners will have Scorpio, Cancer and Aquarius Star Signs or Venus Signs?

Venus in Leo

Lust for life is not your problem. You're into love, good times and creativity in equal amounts, and you have a lot to give in all three areas. Sometimes you live your life like a film, or a television mini-series. You know you do—you can almost watch yourself, watching yourself. Occasionally, everything's just a drama in love. It's better than being bored, though. Some couples are so drab, predictable and ordinary they make you want to hurl yourself off the balcony. Little scenes are not uncommon with you, in love, at work, with friends, or with the family. You also like being around people and events with a bit of an ooh-ah-wow factor. You need a man you can link arms with and look good with. Is it his talent, job, looks, cash or reputation? You adore luxury. You don't care about saving money; you'd rather have Chanel, Prada or The Ritz every time.

What's in your bedroom? The kinds of little luxuries Hollywood stars and English royals probably get for Christmas.

Get his horoscope done! If he's got planets in Aries, Leo or Sagittarius—Ping!

Get him into bed: Turn it into a little saga, give it a bit of style, suspense or drama.

Women like you: Coco Chanel, Jacqueline Kennedy Onassis, Courtney Love, Madonna, Lady Penelope, Nancy Mitford.

Venus in Virgo

If a job's worth doing, it's worth doing perfectly well. You love the details of the work you do, or the papers you pile up on the desk. Getting it right, in a precise and perfect way, is extremely satisfying. Others jam the last piece of the jigsaw into place and make it fit. It looks ugly, and you hate that. You patiently sort and file until you find the right piece, and then . . . perfection. Sex can be like that with you, too. It's nice if it's down to a precision art sometimes. You also get a lot from helping people and quietly doing things for them in a practical way. If you love a man, you probably can't help him enough. If it's a work thing as well, then even better. You understand. You don't mind getting involved—after all, if there's one thing you appreciate, it's the all-important nature of work. Because you want perfection so much, in so many ways, you can get too picky, too critical and too analytical with the poor old human beings around you—and yourself. It doesn't have to be like that, though. You love a routine, and most Venus in Virgo women have little daily rules and rituals about healthy eating and drinking.

What's in your bedroom? A clean smell, and crisp bed linen. A definite absence of dust.
Get his horoscope done! If he's got planets in Taurus, Virgo or Capricorn—Ping!
Get him into bed: Ask him about his work, offer him a practical piece of help or a useful favor.
Women like you: Miss Moneypenny (James Bond's PA), Claudia Schiffer, Shirley Conran, Lois Lane.

Venus in Libra

You know what looks good, and if it doesn't look good, you're probably too nice to say anything, but you quietly die inside. This applies to clothes, houses, art . . . you name it. Your ears are also sensitive (which may reveal itself during sex) and music moves you. You're a mirror-hopper. If you're going out somewhere important and you're not quite sure about the shoes, or the hair, or the jacket (how many times has that happened?), you hop from mirror to mirror throughout the evening. Other people don't notice—they're too busy being charmed by you. You can turn it on, and that's OK. Some people race toward conversational crashes, but you spot the danger zone ten miles before it happens and smoothly swerve everything away from the trouble spot. Born with this Venus sign, you can truly never get enough of love and romance. In your own life, in other people's lives, in films, in poems, in endless reruns of *Pride and Prejudice* on TV . . . You crave the balance that comes when people can be peaceful with each other. That's true beauty. And you love a true working partnership, either in your career or your private life. You especially enjoy it when you balance someone else out with your differences, and vice versa.

What's in your bedroom? Photographs or paintings. Wardrobe contents to die for.

Get his horoscope done! Has he got planets in Gemini, Libra or Aquarius? Ping!

Get him into bed: Send him flowers. Do something old-fashioned and girlie; wear lace or roses.
Women like you: Dawn French, Jayne Torvill, Olivia Newton-John, Linda McCartney, Susan Sarandon.

Venus in Scorpio

People never tell you what nice weather we're having, because they sense something in your eyes that would kill them at five paces. You were made for more than polite conversation or meaningless social crapola. You are an extremely intense, emotional and passionate woman. Relationships bring it out, like the sun luring a tiger snake from its burrow. You go very, very deep with people. The love is several hundred leagues below the sea; the sex resonates inside a dark and moist echo chamber; the hatred (well, you do hate) is earthquake-level. Other people like boring happy endings. You tend not to believe in them. You know about the blood, tears, sweat, vomit, rage, pain, ecstasy and orgasmic highs instead. You dig deeply into life, and it sometimes digs back. You can carry too much poison, and you know it. But nobody understands human nature better. You could write a book about sex, alone. But you never would. You're far too private. Sometimes only really passionate music or poetry can contain and express the enormous power and depth of your emotions, especially where love is concerned.

What's in your bedroom? Black lingerie, dim lights, intense novels about sex, death, power, the occult or revenge.

Get his horoscope done! Does he have planets in Cancer, Scorpio or Pisces? Ping!

Get him into bed: Scorch his pants off with your eyes. Lick your lips and look away a lot.

Women like you: Marianne Faithfull, k.d. lang, Demi Moore, Julia Roberts, Anne Rice, Cruella De Vil (when you have PMS).

Venus in Sagittarius

You know what and who you believe in, and it could be anything from a philosophy of life you've made up yourself to something more formal—like reincarnation, or heaven and hell, or socialism. You have your code, and that's it. Occasionally people get a free lecture, but you mean well. You're funny, or can appreciate other people being funny. You need to have adventures in your life, or to go exploring, to really feel as if you're following your heart. Staying stuck in a rut for security's sake is not you. As you get older, the search for a sense of meaning, and for meaningful relationships, matters more. You don't like the idea that the world is some big, random place. You're always looking for the true explanation, no matter if it's religious, cosmic, scientific or spiritual. When you were younger, you typically fooled around, horsed around and fell out of bed a lot. You really adore travel, and people from other countries. The day you discover hotmail (www.hotmail.com on the Internet) is the day you discover pure heaven. How many friends or potential lovers in how many countries can you actually have?

What's in your bedroom? A travel bag that still hasn't been fully unpacked. Travel books or brochures.

Get his horoscope done! Has he got planets in Aries, Leo or Sagittarius? Ping!

Get him into bed: Tell him a joke, exaggerate a story, rave about your favourite place in the world.

Women like you: Bette Midler, Kaz Cooke, Meg Ryan, Karen Blixen, Maggie O'Connell in *Northern Exposure*.

Venus in Capricorn

There is a part of you that is so solid, so grounded, so normal and so sensible that people could drug you, dress you up in floppy bunny ears and spin you around, and you'd still seem worryingly sane and down to earth. You are particularly serious about love and relationships. It can cause you pain, but you are wise enough to know that pain is just another word for experience, and you can't have a mature or seasoned relationship without it. You like to know where you stand, basically. This philosophy guides you in love, in life and in most things you enjoy. What's the story? You have an built-in BS detector, which is why the more insane Paris fashions leave you cold, and people with pre-tensions turn you off. You're not particularly spontaneous or outrageous, but that's okay. Like-minded people find you eventually, and that's basically what you're after. You love success, no matter whether it's scoring points at the coolest function in town, or pulling off an amazing career coup.

What's in your bedroom? Bits and pieces from work, old or antique things.

Get his horoscope done! Does he have planets in Taurus, Virgo or Capricorn? Ping!

Get him into bed: Play by the rules of the situation, keep your dignity, be cool about it.
Women like you: Sharon Stone, Maggie Tabberer, Cindy Crawford, Tess McGill in *Working Girl.*

Venus in Aquarius

You love people and ideas which are alternative, different or out there. You're instinctively drawn to astrology, for example. You may also enjoy the Internet. You love your network of friends, and you have a lot of them—nothing too emotional, close or complicated, though. You certainly don't have a problem with platonic male-female friendships. Where love is concerned, you appreciate a relationship where you both have your own space and independence. If it feels cool, free, intelligent, feminist and progressive, then you'll go for it. You have unusual tastes and interests by other people's standards, and your wardrobe, home or haircut might reflect this. You can live with uncertainty and weirdness in your love life if it means you still get electricity and excitement. When you go to an art gallery or a shopping plaza you tend to find yourself preferring the bits and pieces nobody else likes—either that or you just walk out!

What's in your bedroom? Things that are in no other woman's bedroom on Earth.

Get his horoscope done! Has he got planets in Gemini, Libra or Aquarius? Ping!

Get him into bed: Be original, be cool, be different, be yourself, shock him a bit.

Women like you: Dame Edna Everage, Germaine Greer, Kate Bush, Gloria Steinem, Lieutenant Uhura in *Star Trek*.

Venus in Pisces

You can take emotional or physical pain away from people and animals, and that's a good thing. If you couldn't do that, you'd probably have to crawl away somewhere. You are so intensely sensitive—not only in terms of your own headspace, but also other people's—that you bruise very easily. There are two ways around this. Either you can soothe suffering away, or you simply have to escape. It doesn't have to involve a lot of money; sometimes all you have to do is daydream, or light some incense. A complete fantasy voyage is something you periodically need to spend money on, though. Your imagination and your idealism are strong, and can get you into serious trouble with men. Sometimes the fact that you wear blinkers is a lovely thing, as it lets you accept men with all their faults and still love them. At other times you can almost feel crucified over it. A bit of balance in your life is a good thing. Poetry, art, photography or music are superb channels. You may also be drawn to the spiritual or psychic side of life.

What's in your bedroom? Impractical but intensely wonderful objects. Fabulous fabrics. Arty photographs.
Get his horoscope done! Does he have planets in Cancer, Scorpio, Pisces? Ping!
Get him into bed: Read his mind in a sympathetic way. Flutter your fingers on his arm.
Women like you: Joy Adamson, Elizabeth Taylor, Jilly Cooper, Anaïs Nin, The Little Mermaid.

SIX

Profile of Your Soulmate

Look up your date and year of birth in the tables to find out your soulmate profile. For example, if you were born on 6 January 1960, when Mars was in the sign of Sagittarius, your soulmate is an explorer; if you were born on 16 January 1960, after Mars had moved into Capricorn, then your soulmate is an achiever. If your birthday falls outside the years shown in these tables, check out www.astro.com on the Internet—it'll give you a free rundown of all your planets.

No matter when your birthday is, though, there are certain qualities you will always identify with in men. Because you are a Gemini, some of your ideas about what a "real" man is are based on your Star Sign. He has to be a good talker, thinker or writer, for a start. He'll have to have wit, or a funny way of looking at the world—nothing too heavy. Men who aren't so bright, quick or sharp about life may not really seem like "true" men to you. Chances are, your ex-boyfriends or your current partner has some of these qualities:

- *A healthy sense of humor*
- *A way with words, either on paper or in person*
- *Cunning or intelligence—he uses both*
- *A fundamental curiosity about everybody and everything*

To discover the sort of man who really is a part of you, though, explore this next section. Add these qualities to the traits you've just read about, and you'll begin to get an accurate picture of your astrological soulmate.

1949

MTH	DAY	SIGN
JAN	1	CAP
JAN	4	AQU
FEB	11	PIS
MAR	21	ARI
APR	30	TAU
JUN	10	GEM
JUL	23	CAN
SEP	7	LEO
OCT	27	VIR
DEC	26	LIB

1950

MTH	DAY	SIGN
JAN	1	LIB
MAR	28	VIR
JUN	11	LIB
AUG	10	SCO
SEP	25	SAG
NOV	6	CAP
DEC	15	AQU

1951

MTH	DAY	SIGN
JAN	1	AQU
JAN	22	PIS
MAR	1	ARI
APR	10	TAU
MAY	21	GEM
JUL	3	CAN
AUG	18	LEO
OCT	5	VIR
NOV	24	LIB

1952

MTH	DAY	SIGN
JAN	1	LIB
JAN	20	SCO
AUG	27	SAG
OCT	12	CAP
NOV	21	AQU
DEC	30	PIS

1953

MTH	DAY	SIGN
JAN	1	PIS
FEB	8	ARI
MAR	20	TAU
MAY	1	GEM
JUN	14	CAN
JUL	29	LEO
SEP	14	VIR
NOV	1	LIB
DEC	20	SCO

1954

MTH	DAY	SIGN
JAN	1	SCO
FEB	9	SAG
APR	12	CAP
JUL	3	SAG
AUG	24	CAP
OCT	21	AQU
DEC	4	PIS

1955

MTH	DAY	SIGN
JAN	1	AQU
JAN	5	PIS
FEB	2	ARI
MAR	14	TAU
MAR	31	ARI
JUN	5	TAU
JUL	7	GEM
OCT	13	LIB
NOV	29	SCO

1956

MTH	DAY	SIGN
JAN	1	SCO
JAN	14	SAG
FEB	28	CAP
APR	14	AQU
JUN	3	PIS
DEC	6	ARI

1957

MTH	DAY	SIGN
JAN	1	ARI
JAN	28	TAU
MAR	17	GEM
MAY	4	CAN
JUN	21	LEO
AUG	8	VIR
SEP	24	LIB
NOV	8	SCO
DEC	23	SAG

1958

MTH	DAY	SIGN
JAN	1	SAG
FEB	3	CAP
MAR	17	AQU
APR	27	PIS
JUN	7	ARI
JUL	21	TAU
SEP	21	GEM
OCT	29	TAU

1959

MTH	DAY	SIGN
JAN	1	TAU
FEB	10	GEM
APR	10	CAN
JUN	1	LEO
JUL	20	VIR
SEP	5	LIB
OCT	21	SCO
DEC	3	SAG

1960

MTH	DAY	SIGN
JAN	1	SAG
JAN	14	CAP
FEB	23	AQU
APR	2	PIS
MAY	11	ARI
JUN	20	TAU
AUG	2	GEM
SEP	21	CAN

1961

MTH	DAY	SIGN
JAN	1	CAN
FEB	5	GEM
FEB	7	CAN
MAY	6	LEO
JUN	28	VIR
AUG	17	LIB
OCT	1	SCO
NOV	13	SAG
DEC	24	CAP

1962

MTH	DAY	SIGN
JAN	1	CAP
FEB	1	AQU
MAR	12	PIS
APR	19	ARI
MAY	28	TAU
JUL	9	GEM
AUG	22	CAN
OCT	11	LEO

1963

MTH	DAY	SIGN
JAN	1	LEO
JUN	3	VIR
JUL	27	LIB
SEP	12	SCO
OCT	25	SAG
DEC	5	CAP

1964

MTH	DAY	SIGN
JAN	1	CAP
JAN	13	AQU
FEB	20	PIS
MAR	29	ARI
MAY	7	TAU
JUN	17	GEM
JUL	30	CAN
SEP	15	LEO
NOV	6	VIR

1965

MTH	DAY	SIGN
JAN	1	VIR
JUN	29	LIB
AUG	20	SCO
OCT	4	SAG
NOV	14	CAP
DEC	23	AQU

1966

MTH	DAY	SIGN
JAN	1	AQU
JAN	30	PIS
MAR	9	ARI
APR	17	TAU
MAY	28	GEM
JUL	11	CAN
AUG	25	LEO
OCT	12	VIR
DEC	4	LIB

1967

MTH	DAY	SIGN
JAN	1	LIB
FEB	12	SCO
MAR	31	LIB
JUL	19	SCO
SEP	10	SAG
OCT	23	CAP
DEC	1	AQU

1968

MTH	DAY	SIGN
JAN	1	AQU
JAN	9	PIS
FEB	17	ARI
MAR	27	TAU
MAY	8	GEM
JUN	21	CAN
AUG	5	LEO
SEP	21	VIR
NOV	9	LIB
DEC	29	SCO

1969

MTH	DAY	SIGN
JAN	1	SCO
FEB	25	SAG
SEP	21	CAP
NOV	4	AQU
DEC	15	PIS

1970

MTH	DAY	SIGN
JAN	1	PIS
JAN	24	ARI
MAR	7	TAU
APR	18	GEM
JUN	2	CAN
JUL	18	LEO
SEP	3	VIR
OCT	20	LIB
DEC	6	SCO

1971

MTH	DAY	SIGN
JAN	1	SCO
JAN	23	SAG
MAR	12	CAP
MAY	3	AQU
NOV	6	PIS
DEC	26	ARI

1972

MTH	DAY	SIGN
JAN	1	ARI
FEB	10	TAU
MAR	27	GEM
MAY	12	CAN
JUN	28	LEO
AUG	15	VIR
SEP	30	LIB
NOV	15	SCO
DEC	30	SAG

1973

MTH	DAY	SIGN
JAN	1	SAG
FEB	12	CAP
MAR	26	AQU
MAY	8	PIS
JUN	20	ARI
AUG	12	TAU
OCT	29	ARI
DEC	24	TAU

1974

MTH	DAY	SIGN
JAN	1	TAU
FEB	27	GEM
APR	20	CAN
JUN	9	LEO
JUL	27	VIR
SEP	12	LIB
OCT	28	SCO
DEC	10	SAG

1975

MTH	DAY	SIGN
JAN	1	SAG
JAN	21	CAP
MAR	3	AQU
APR	11	PIS
MAY	21	ARI
JUL	1	TAU
AUG	14	GEM
OCT	17	CAN
NOV	25	GEM

1976

MTH	DAY	SIGN
JAN	1	GEM
MAR	18	CAN
MAY	15	LEO
JUL	7	VIR
AUG	4	LIB
OCT	9	SCO
NOV	21	SAG
DEC	12	CAP

1977

MTH	DAY	SIGN
JAN	1	CAP
FEB	9	AQU
MAR	20	PIS
APR	27	ARI
JUN	6	TAU
JUL	17	GEM
SEP	1	CAN
OCT	26	LEO

1978

MTH	DAY	SIGN
JAN	1	LEO
JAN	26	CAN
APR	10	LEO
JUN	14	VIR
AUG	4	LIB
SEP	19	SCO
NOV	2	SAG
DEC	12	CAP

1979

MTH	DAY	SIGN
JAN	1	CAP
JAN	20	AQU
FEB	27	PIS
APR	7	ARI
MAY	16	TAU
JUN	26	GEM
AUG	8	CAN
SEP	24	LEO
NOV	19	VIR

1980

MTH	DAY	SIGN
JAN	1	VIR
MAR	11	LEO
MAY	4	VIR
JUL	10	LIB
AUG	29	SCO
OCT	12	SAG
NOV	22	CAP
DEC	30	AQU

1981

MTH	DAY	SIGN
JAN	1	AQU
FEB	6	PIS
MAR	17	ARI
APR	25	TAU
JUN	5	GEM
JUL	18	CAN
SEP	2	LEO
OCT	21	VIR
DEC	16	LIB

1982

MTH	DAY	SIGN
JAN	1	LIB
AUG	3	SCO
SEP	20	SAG
OCT	31	CAP
DEC	10	AQU

1983

MTH	DAY	SIGN
JAN	1	AQU
JAN	17	PIS
FEB	25	ARI
APR	5	TAU
MAY	16	GEM
JUN	29	CAN
AUG	13	LEO
SEP	30	VIR
NOV	18	LIB

1984

MTH	DAY	SIGN
JAN	1	LIB
JAN	11	SCO
AUG	17	SAG
OCT	5	CAP
NOV	15	AQU
DEC	25	PIS

You have . . .	Your soulmate is a . . .
Mars in Aries	☆ go-getter
Mars in Taurus	☆ rock
Mars in Gemini	☆ communicator
Mars in Cancer	☆ caretaker
Mars in Leo	☆ star
Mars in Virgo	☆ thinker
Mars in Libra	☆ balancer
Mars in Scorpio	☆ depth charge
Mars in Sagittarius	☆ explorer
Mars in Capricorn	☆ achiever
Mars in Aquarius	☆ individual
Mars in Pisces	☆ dreamer

Go-Getter

- **Let's face it:** He has drive and energy. He's an action man, either at work, or on the weekends. He has loads of initiative. He's not afraid of people or situations which might intimidate other people. He can't survive without challenges to keep him going. He's masculine, in the old-fashioned sense of the word. He never gives up, or gives in. He doesn't hang around. He doesn't waste any time. In a word, he has balls. He'll never walk away from a fight or an argument—backing down makes him feel sick.

- **Why you'll love this side of him:** It's a turn-on, basically. He had the wimp part of his brain extracted before he was born. You'll know exactly what's going on with him, because he's in or out of situations so quickly. His male energy is extremely sexy.
- **Why you'll loathe this side of him:** He's incredibly pushy. Why doesn't he just let up sometimes? He can be an absolute bastard in an argument. He lacks patience and sensitivity just when you need it most. He basically puts himself first—all too often.
- **What you tell your friends:** "He doesn't waste any time."

Rock

- **Let's face it:** He calms you down. He's so down to earth about life. No pretensions. No wacky ideas about things. He takes his time. He makes life seem settled and normal. He brings in the money, or puts up the shelves, or sorts out the garden. He's like a good massage at the end of a stressful day. He understands money, but he also has a straight sense of ethics, morals and values. He appreciates fine workmanship and beautiful places and objects.

- **Why you'll love this side of him:** He's soothing company. He's in no hurry. There is something concrete, solid and secure about him. He has money in the bank, his own home or a stable lifestyle. When he tells you that you're looking good, you know it's true.
- **Why you'll loathe this side of him:** He can be the world's most boring plodder. He can get stuck in a rut and keep you there, too. He can be so into money, houses, business or possessions that you wonder if there's more to life. He's too swayed by appearances.
- **What you tell your friends:** "He's nice and he's normal."

Communicator

- **Let's face it:** You'll never be bored. He's quick on the uptake. He's funny, too. And he gives great phone, writes the best letters and lends you amazing books. He's scarily intelligent, and he can make you laugh when life gets too heavy or serious. He can usually tell you the latest news headlines, or at least the latest dirt on people. He's a mine of information, but he's never dull about it. He's fast and sharp, well informed and a natural reader, writer, talker or thinker.

- **Why you'll love this side of him:** He's entertaining. He actually applies his brain to things, and you'll either want to tape-record the phone messages or save the love letters in a bank safe. You can imagine him being switched on, funny and intelligent at the age of 70.
- **Why you'll loathe this side of him:** When he stops being clever about everything, he just sounds totally superficial and shallow. And there are times when you wish he would switch off his whirring brain and feel something with a bit more true soul.
- **What you tell your friends:** "Let me read you what he put on my Valentine's Day card."

Caretaker

- **Let's face it:** He turns houses or apartments into real homes. He has a good, strong relationship with at least one family member—maybe more. It's part of the reason he has such a caring nature. He doesn't waste money. But even so, he's into people—not things. He can be sweet and sympathetic, like a human Band-Aid. He's walking proof that you don't have to be a SNAG (Sensitive New Age Guy) in order to be sensitive. He actually cares.

- **Why you'll love this side of him:** He's even sweet when he sulks. He knows why families are important, and takes children or parenthood seriously, whether he's into it or not. He's extremely emotional, and he's more in touch with his feelings than other men.
- **Why you'll loathe this side of him:** He can become overly attached to one of four things—his home, his mother, his country or his family. To you, it just looks like he's clinging to something. His irrational moods and feelings are all emotion and no brains.
- **What you tell your friends:** "He'd make a great father."

Star

- **Let's face it:** He is respected and admired. He is a legend in his own lunchtime—and a few other people's. He has strong leadership qualities or powerful self-expression. As a result of this, he tends to shine—and also to stand out. He doesn't lack confidence. In fact, his ego sometimes blows out. He has what it takes to tell other people what to do. He may also have the ability to create, perform or entertain. He has style. He has class.

- **Why you'll love this side of him:** He's special. A leader of men, or even slightly famous. Everyone's heard of him. You respect him. He makes you look good. He's the kind of man you can genuinely look up to. And he doesn't have a confidence problem—thank God.
- **Why you'll loathe this side of him:** He can be so arrogant you want to walk out on him. And the drama! He can turn the smallest thing into a three-act play. He's quite self-involved, and wants the bathroom mirror when you do. And—yes—he can be a jerk.
- **What you tell your friends:** "He's not short on confidence."

Thinker

- **Let's face it:** He's efficient and smart. He has his home life or work life sorted out. Part of it's down to the fact that he's always making lists. But he also finds it easy to get his head around things. He's smart, he's in control. He doesn't boast about it, but he has the kind of brain that computers will never copy. He's helpful. He's reliable. You know where you are with him. He takes care of his health. He's completely responsible.

- **Why you'll love this side of him:** He's very careful and methodical, which you like to see in a man. He takes good care of his body, his workplace and his life. He's impressively intelligent. If you've been with drifters or dreamers, he's the antidote.
- **Why you'll loathe this side of him:** He can be ridiculously picky and critical, taking one detail about you, or your behavior, or your life, and treating it like a major problem. He can be irritatingly boring about the small details of life, fussing around with trivial things.
- **What you tell your friends:** "He's totally reliable."

Balancer

- **Let's face it:** He is very good at keeping your relationship evenly balanced, and will usually compromise to avoid an argument. If you ever actually fight, he won't have a problem with making the peace. His taste in clothes, music, art or homes is very important to him. He is naturally quite charming and diplomatic with people, and he's safe to take anywhere, from your parents' place to a rave. He has a talent for getting along with people—and for relationships.

- **Why you'll love this side of him:** He believes in flowers, and he actually watches the close-up scenes in romantic films. He can relate to *Romeo and Juliet.* He cares about the way he dresses and how he gets his hair cut. He also appreciates your style or taste.
- **Why you'll loathe this side of him:** This man can be the original fence-sitter, never actually expressing an opinion in case it makes him unpopular with someone. Sometimes he can seem fake, especially on a social level. Charm is fine, but he can take it too far.
- **What you tell your friends:** "Guess what he did for my birthday!"

Depth Charge

- **Let's face it:** He's a passionate man. He feels things very deeply, and is intense about what and who he loves—and what and who he hates! He has quite a bit of power or magnetism about him. And sexually inane terms like "shagging" or "bonking" don't apply. Sex is not trivial to him. It's about a deep, emotional and powerful connection which goes way beyond the physical. He's a fairly secretive, closed person. That can be quite sexy, too.

- **Why you'll love this side of him:** He's got soul. He's not a boy, he's a man. He burns for things, and you love it. He truly understands life in all its gory detail, and doesn't mind facing extreme situations or emotions with you. He's a powerful and influential person.
- **Why you'll loathe this side of him:** His dark side is ten times as black as any other man's. He can be manipulative—a real power tripper, in fact. It may come out at work, or (worst-case scenario) in his private life. He can be ridiculously obsessive about things.
- **What you tell your friends:** "Sex with him is . . ."

Explorer

- **Let's face it:** He's into the big picture. He likes traveling to other countries, or exploring the great outdoors, or getting out of the house and into more interesting experiences. He's funny, too—his sense of humor is healthy. There is nothing narrow-minded or petty about this guy. He has the long view of life. He's a bit of a philosopher at heart. He's also drawn to friendships with travelers, foreigners or people who've studied quite widely.

- **Why you'll love this side of him:** You could have a lot of fun taking off to Asia or Europe together. He's game for most things. He has the right angle on life, too. He never takes it too seriously. His horizons are broader than most men's, and that's sexy.
- **Why you'll loathe this side of him:** You'd probably prefer it if he spent less time gazing at the next horizon, and a little more time on the small stuff—like security, intimacy, your feelings, and all the practical details of life. And sometimes his jokes aren't funny.
- **What you tell your friends:** "He has the most amazing attitude towards life."

Achiever

- **Let's face it:** He's a heavyweight. He's more mature than a lot of the guys around him, and he's got a wise, experienced quality. No wonder his career to date has been such a success story. He's prepared to wait for what he wants. And he's also prepared to work hard. He's straight-up and serious, and that can be quite sexy, because you will instinctively feel like getting him to loosen up—preferably in bed.
- **Why you'll love this side of him:** There's a lot to

admire about this man. He gets to the top by doing things the old-fashioned way. He has a lot of wisdom and experience, and that's something you can respect. He makes you feel safe. You know where you stand.

- **Why you'll loathe this side of him:** His ambitions—both in career terms and socially—are quite high. You could get awfully sick of watching his social game-playing with "useful" people, or hearing about work politics. You might find he's hung up on status, too.
- **What you tell your friends:** "He's got it together."

Individual

- **Let's face it:** He's one of a kind. He's not very good at fitting in for the sake of it. He might look different from other people, or just be extremely different on the inside. He's exciting to be around. You'll feel a definite buzz when you're with him. He's also a man ahead of his time, in many ways. What he's into now, everyone else will be into next year. He doesn't fake it, or compromise. He's his own person, and he's an absolute original.
- **Why you'll love this side of him:** He's very

broad-minded and progressive about life. He understands feminism and has a basically decent, admirable, humanitarian view of the world. He's electrifying company. And he has a dash of genius.

- **Why you'll loathe this side of him:** Mad, mad, mad. Sometimes he can be so stubbornly different and weird. If you go left, he'll go right. If everyone's going north, he'll go south. You feel like kicking him! Then there are his funny little ways—they're not always funny.
- **What you tell your friends:** "He's one of a kind."

Dreamer

- **Let's face it:** He's sensitive. He's raw like sushi. He is emotional or psychic, or both at the same time. He can relate to music, poetry, photography or films in a profound way because of this sensitivity. He's not afraid to make sacrifices for other people. And you don't have to explain how you're feeling to him—he just seems to know instinctively. He can't handle too much reality. He needs to drift off, dream or escape.
- **Why you'll love this side of him:** At last, a man with feelings! He's hard to catch or pin down

sometimes, but like a half-remembered song, you'll be happily haunted by him. He's kind and compassionate. He can feel for a hurt woman, or a hurt butterfly. He's soft inside.

- **Why you'll loathe this side of him:** You know that song "Reality Used to Be a Friend of Mine"? You can probably relate to it if you're with this guy. Drink or drugs may not bring out the best in him. But his worst faults are vagueness, hopelessness and chaotic life mess!
- **What you tell your friends:** "He feels what I'm feeling."

SEVEN

The Spooky Bit at the Back

Over the years, my job as an astrologer has given me the chance to explore other New Age ideas as well. Some of them work, some of them don't. I met Shirley MacLaine once. I asked her if there was anything in the New Age she didn't believe. She shook her head and said she believed in *everything*. I don't. But here are some quick tips and spooky solutions that I've road-tested over the last ten years. They've got nothing to do with astrology, but they really work!

Feng Shui Your Bedroom

Have you been waiting on money for months? Is someone at work driving you insane? Do you want to go to Morocco but have no idea how you'll manage it? Try feng shui (say it "fong-shoy").

You can feng shui your whole house or apartment if you wish, but for a quick fix, begin with your bedroom. The first thing you will need to do is get rid of any mess, junk or unwanted objects. Here are some classic examples:

- *Clothes that need mending that you've shoved under the bed*
- *Dead or dying plants*
- *Photos of ex-boyfriends, old letters, receipts, bills and other bits of paper*
- *Compact discs or tapes you never play*
- *Magazines and newspapers*
- *Books you've never got around to reading*
- *Unwanted presents you feel guilty about throwing out*
- *Empty perfume bottles, half-empty jars of moisturizer*
- *Keys belonging to houses, apartments and cars from years ago*
- *Rolled-up posters in the corner*

Karen Kingston, author of *Clear Your Clutter With Feng Shui* and *Creating Sacred Space With Feng Shui,* is an expert on this stuff. If you'd like to go the whole hog, and also clear the old vibes and stale energy from your bedroom, use her special rituals—which include clapping, ringing bells, lighting candles, burning incense, sprinkling holy water and offering flowers and prayers.

For more information on this, see Karen's web site at www.spaceclearing.com.

The general idea of starting with a clean, uncluttered space is very important to feng shui. There is no point in sticking a crystal in your money corner if it's going to sit there with an old pet rock and a 1982 *Dynasty* calendar. Be ruthless with every object in your room. Here's what to do:

1. *Look at it.*
2. *Does it bring your energy down or up?*
3. *If it brings you down, imagine the accumulated "sagging" effect of seeing this thing ten times a day, 365 days a year.*

It may be the only photograph you have of the guy you spent two years of your life with, but if every time you see it you feel an energy drop, rip it up.

After the de-junking comes the boring bit. The vacuuming, the mending and the window-washing. Then comes the slightly more interesting bit—visual cleaning.

Sit on the floor. Imagine a dazzling white light pouring in through the light fixture on the ceiling, and filling the entire room. This is your universal cleaner. More powerful than Mr. Clean, it's superb for obliterating old vibes, bad vibes, and indifferent vibes. Make sure the light is as bright, white and pure as you can make it.

Make sure you see it going under the bed and into the corners.

When you've finished, open the windows wide. You have just moved an awful lot of stuck, stale bedroom energy. A few people have told me that wonderful and strange things start happening just on the strength of this junk-chuck, cleanup and white-light exercise. Phones ring with job offers. Badly behaved boyfriends turn up with flowers. Party invitations land in the mailbox.

Now for the fun part. Look at the plan of your bedroom opposite.

What area of your life do you want to focus on? That's where you decorate, put flowers, light candles, burn incense or aromatherapy oil. That's where you hang a picture or photograph of something that makes you happy, or something which sums up what you'd like to see happening.

You can also do some problem-solving by avoiding the big feng shui no-nos:

1. *Don't have your feet pointing at the door from the bed.*
2. *Don't have a mirror facing you when you're in bed.*
3. *If there's a fan in the room, move your bed so you're not sleeping under the blades.*

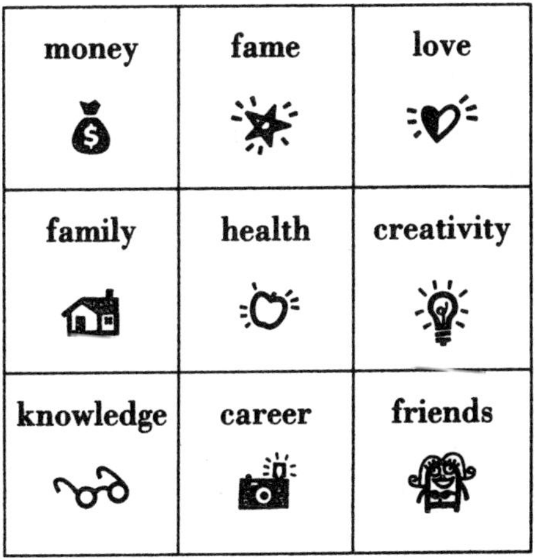

money	fame	love
family	health	creativity
knowledge	career	friends

The doorway is on this side of your room

People tie themselves into knots if their bedroom isn't a neat square or oblong. If you have a corner of the room missing (in an L-shaped bedroom, for example) don't panic. Just do what you can to dress up where that corner should be. If your money corner is missing, that's where you could put a beautiful vase on the floor, and fill it with the best flowers you can afford every week. If your love corner is missing, put a rose quartz crystal in there. Some people hang mirrors on the wall of the L-shaped bit to give the illusion that the space really does extend.

It's all about using your imagination, and your common sense. If you don't want to be single, don't put up a Picasso print of a single woman in your love corner!

I've known people to see results on the same day, and other people within a few weeks. I sorted out my office and moved stacks of my first novel, *Single White E-mail,* out of cardboard boxes and into my creativity corner. The book had dropped off the best-seller lists two months previously and I honestly thought that its time was over, which is probably why I'd stashed it away in boxes. Within three days of putting it in pride of place in my creativity corner, it zoomed back onto the best-seller list at number six.

Start small, with your bedroom. If good things begin to happen for you, I recommend you go all the way and do your entire house and garden, or your apartment. Karen Kingston and Lillian Too have both written great books on the subject.

Call a Psychic Cab

This works for me about nine times out of ten. You may find it happens ten times out of ten for you! The next time you are desperate for a cab, stand on the curb and send this silent message out into the streets:

"I am (here) and I want to go (there). I have (x) dollars. I can wait for (x) minutes."

This works if it's raining, if everybody is lining up on the road in front of you, and even if it's 3 P.M. and there are no cabs on the road. Once, I didn't get a cab within my specified time (five minutes) but a friend "happened" to drive past and gave me a lift instead. It helps if you visualize the cab pulling up in front of you, and you happily getting in.

Take An Aura Shower

This is good if you're feeling tired, stressed out, ill or otherwise fed up. If you do it properly you will feel the following within twenty minutes:

- *Peace of mind*
- *Mild bliss*

I have watched people do this experiment, and some of them start smiling for no apparent reason. Other people have told me that they settle down and feel a bit more normal about life when they try it.

Lie down on the bed, or on the floor. Flop. Take

three deep breaths. Flop again. Don't feel stupid or anxious about this. It's easy. Next, say these words in your head: "What color do I need?" The rule for this is—first thought, best thought! Don't agonize over it. Zoom in on the precise shade of that color. If you chose blue, do you mean turquoise blue, or deep purple-blue?

Imagine that you have amazing rings on all your fingers, inlaid with jewels in that color. See yourself wearing that color. Take a bath in it. Feel it inside your body, as well as outside it. Stay with the color for as long as you like. This is when some people start smiling involuntarily, while others find themselves letting out a long sigh, much to their surprise. This is a sign that the aura shower is working.

Ask again: "What color do I need?" If nothing comes up, you only needed one color to correct your aura, and you can get up and carry on with your day. But you may get another color, and another color, and so on. Continue until you feel you're finished.

Wish Books

Buy a notebook you really like. On a separate piece of scrap paper, write down a list of what you would like to happen in your life. Put in a lot of details. If you want to sketch something to show what you mean, then do that. Really think about what you're after. If you want a man who has a hairy chest and a wooden leg, write it down. Nobody else is going to see this, so what have you got to lose?

Using the scrap paper gives you a chance to be absolutely sure about what you want when you finally glue things, write things or draw things in your wish book. This is a special book, which will help to bring many (if not all) of your wishes about. So keep it clean, make sure it looks great, and hide it in a safe place.

Some people cut out photographs from magazines and stick them in their wish books. Others draw what they want. Feel free to add some of the details or notes you worked out on your scrap paper.

The rule with wish books is, if it's for the good of you and the people around you, it will probably happen. What you're after is a win-win situation. Let's say you've cut out a picture of Nelson Mandela (for his integrity) and a picture of Brad Pitt (for his dimples), in your quest to dream up the ideal man. If a guy like this happens to be out there and also looking for someone like you, you'll meet.

If, on the other hand, your boyfriend has dumped you for no sensible reason, and you cut out a picture of a piranha fish and paste it over a photo of his groin, it's probably not going to happen. Win-win works. Win–

groin mutilation tends to do nothing except create bad karma for you.

Here's a list of some of the things that have been wished into existence over the years—by people I know, and sometimes by me. Next to each real-life wish book example, I've written the time it took to come true.

- *A white beach house with blue and white tiles on the porch, and a rocking horse in the children's bedroom. (This was cut out of a magazine. It took eight months for the house and the rocking horse to arrive. The blue and white tiles didn't make it, though!)*
- *A pair of black leather pants like Jim Morrison's. (These were found on a market stall about a week later. A classic win-win, as the guy who was selling the pants thought he'd never get rid of them.)*
- *A fun romance in America. (This person got the fun, the romance and America almost two years after drawing a picture of it, complete with love hearts and the Statue of Liberty.)*
- *A career with radio, TV, money, creativity and freedom. (I actually drew this for a friend and she e-mailed me two weeks later with this subject header—!!!!!!!!!!!— to tell me it had happened.)*
- *Two golden retriever puppies with pink ribbons round*

their necks. (OK, I admit it, I cut this out of a magazine and put it in my wish book. About three months later, I was walking past the local noticeboard and saw an advertisement asking for someone with spare time to walk a golden retriever. I did, and Max became one of my favorite canines in the whole world.)

This last example shows something else about wish books— you might get part of the wish, rather than all of it, or it may come about in a surprising way.

Computer Magic

If you have a screen-saver that allows you to make up a sentence and put it on your computer, don't waste it. You can use the same idea behind the wish book, and write down something that you would like to see happen—then watch it roll across your screen on a regular basis. I typed in this sentence in bright pink: PARIS IN THE SPRING. I found myself there last year, so it was definitely worth the effort.

People always ask me how this stuff works. I really don't know, but when you consciously decide to take something out of your head and write it down, draw it, or cut it out and stick it in a book, the universe shifts. It works the other way, too. If you wander around with these ideas in your head—

- *I'm going to have to be lucky to pass my exam*
- *I'm hooked on cigarettes*
- *I always get the weirdos*

—well, does anything ever change?

The only rule with computer magic is your frame of mind when you program your sentence into the machine. If you feel pessimistic, uncertain, silly or embarrassed, it won't work. The best attitude is either: total belief that it's going to happen one day, though you have no idea how; or The Doris Day Approach—what will be, will be. In other words, it would be great if you got what you wanted, but you're not going to sink into despair if it doesn't happen.

The wish book win-win principle also applies to computers. If what you want is fine by other people as well as you, then it stands a better chance of happening. Giving up smoking is a good example—unless you're married to the head of Benson and Hedges, I guess.

Name Your Car

The chicks at Penguin Books swear by this and so do I. If you have trouble with mechanical or high-tech objects—like cars, faxes, computers, laptops, microwave ovens, modems, plug-in aromatherapy burners and so on—name them. Mean what you say. Take your time to choose the name. Use it to communicate with your little mechanical or digital friend frequently. When I was having hassles with my laptop (the screen was wobbling and I was stuck in the country, far away from technical support), I gave it a name. Little Miranda. (The big computer is called Big Miranda.) I talked to Little Miranda and asked her to work for me. She stopped wobbling.

Reading Pizzas

Do you want to see into the future? If tarot cards are a problem for you, and your dreams just aren't predictive, try pizza reading.

First, ask your question. Your psychic side will answer it for you, using symbols, images and ideas which you will see in the pizza. What you see in the cheese, the pepperoni and the mushrooms will be personal to you. If, for example, you see a door key, and that reminds you of your roommate who is always forgetting his key, then that is a reference to him. Let your brain "bounce" around images and ideas in a dreamy way. Make sure you write it all down, though. Time may well reveal that you have answered your own question about the future by what you saw on the day you did your pizza reading.

You can also read clouds. I did it on a long and boring flight from London to Moscow. The question I asked was, "What will I find when I get to Moscow? What experiences will I have?" After a few minutes of staring at the clouds, I wrote down this:

- *A man with a birthmark on his face*
- *Little kids with Hare Krishna ponytails*
- *Lots of dogs*

When we got to Moscow Airport, a man with a port wine birthmark on the left side of his face took our passports. I met the dogs the same night—a pack of hungry mongrels hanging around the hotel trash cans (they howled every night for a week, so they really were a major feature of my stay). The little kids with the Hare Krishna ponytails turned up on the second to last day. They were in front of me in the line for the ATM. Try cloud reading next time you fly—especially if they're not serving pizza.

Get Back to Me on This One

To finish the book, I'd like to try an experiment. Have you got a pen in your bag? Good. Look around the room, or the train, or the bus, or the plane (but hopefully not the car—this is a non-driving exercise).

Let your eyes settle on the first thing you see. It may be something quite boring, like a TV set, or quite detailed, like a piece of embroidery. Even a teacup will do.

Allow yourself to float off. What does this object or thing in front of you bring to mind? Without thinking too hard, write down your impressions in the space that follows—

Don't edit yourself. If you're staring at a manila folder and it reminds you of your teacher at school with a beer gut, who reminds you of Foster's, which reminds you of foster homes, which reminds you of stray dogs, which reminds you of wanting to be a vet, then put it all down.

Now, turn this page upside down.

You have just answered the question "What happy choices are in store for me in the 21st century?"

If you are astounded (or if it comes true), I'd like to hear about it.

Please e-mail me at this address: jessica@zip.com.au.

And have a great millennium!